I Can Draw....
PEOPLE

Artwork by Terry Longhurst

Text by Amanda O'Neill

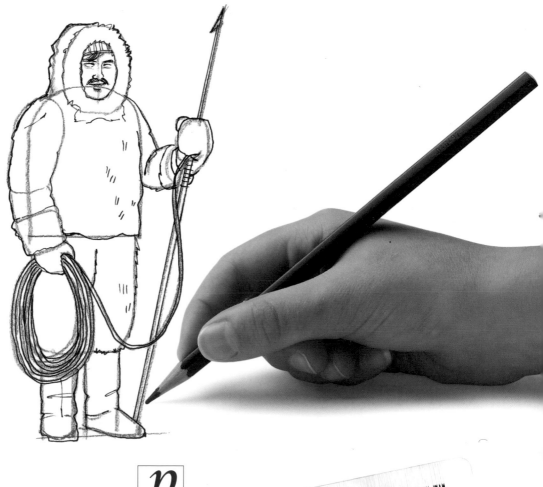

p

This is a Parragon Book
This edition published in 2004

Parragon
Queen Street House
4 Queen Street
Bath BA1 1HE, UK

Copyright © Parragon 2001

Designed, packaged, and produced by
Touchstone

Hardback ISBN 1-40540-354-3
Paperback ISBN 1-40540-038-2

Artwork by Terry Longhurst
Text by Amanda O'Neill
Edited by Philip de Ste. Croix

Printed in China

About this book

Everybody can enjoy drawing, but sometimes it's hard to know where to begin. The subject you want to draw can look very complicated. This book shows you how to start, by breaking down your subject into a series of simple shapes.

The tools you need are very simple. The basic requirements are paper and pencils. Very thin paper wears through if you have to rub out a line, so choose paper that is thick enough to work on. Pencils come with different leads, from very hard to very soft. Very hard pencils give a clean, thin line which is best for finishing drawings. Very soft ones give a thicker, darker line. You will probably find a medium pencil most useful.

If you want to colour in your drawing, you have the choice of paints, coloured inks, or felt-tip pens. Fine felt-tips are useful for drawing outlines, thick felt-tips are better for colouring in.

The most important tool you have is your own eyes. The mistake many people make is to draw what they think something looks like, instead of really looking at it carefully first. Half the secret of making your drawing look good is getting the proportions right. Study your subject before you start, and break it down in your mind into sections. Check how much bigger, or longer, or shorter, one part is than another. Notice where one part joins another, and at what angle. See where there are flowing curves, and where there are straight lines.

The step-by-step drawings in this book show you exactly how to do this. Each subject is broken down into easy stages, so you can build up your drawing one piece at a time. Look carefully at each shape before – and after – you draw it. If you find you have drawn it the wrong size or in the wrong place, correct it before you go on. Then the next shape will fit into place, and piece-by-piece you can build up a fantastic picture.

Boxer

The sport of boxing dates back to Ancient Greek and Roman times. But the rules and padded gloves used today were introduced in the 19th century. Boxers aim to score points by landing punches with the knuckle part of the glove. They may win a bout on points or by knocking out their opponent.

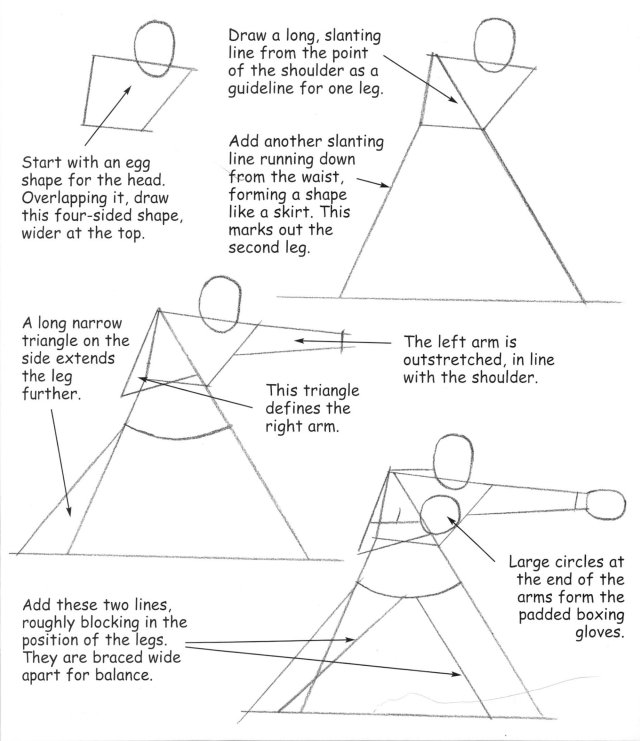

Start with an egg shape for the head. Overlapping it, draw this four-sided shape, wider at the top.

Draw a long, slanting line from the point of the shoulder as a guideline for one leg.

Add another slanting line running down from the waist, forming a shape like a skirt. This marks out the second leg.

A long narrow triangle on the side extends the leg further.

This triangle defines the right arm.

The left arm is outstretched, in line with the shoulder.

Large circles at the end of the arms form the padded boxing gloves.

Add these two lines, roughly blocking in the position of the legs. They are braced wide apart for balance.

Now draw the legs, using the guidelines created earlier. Boxers need strong legs to keep on the move.

Draw the face. The head is tucked in, so as not to offer the chin as a target for the opponent.

The left arm is thrust out in a left jab.

Mark in the boots, which come well up the calf of the leg to provide support.

The right arm is held close to the body ready to strike. Draw slightly bulging curves at the shoulder and down the arms to give the shape of strong muscles.

The weight is taken on the left leg. The right foot is just lifting off the ground.

Boxers don't have to be big men: the different weight classes range from tiny flyweight to mighty heavyweight. But they do have to be very fit. Quick reactions are as important as a powerful punch.

Cowboy

From about 1870 onwards, cattle raising was big business in the Wild West of America – and it all depended on cowboys. They tended the herds, and drove them long distances to markets. Western films make their lives look glamorous, but they worked hard in tough conditions.

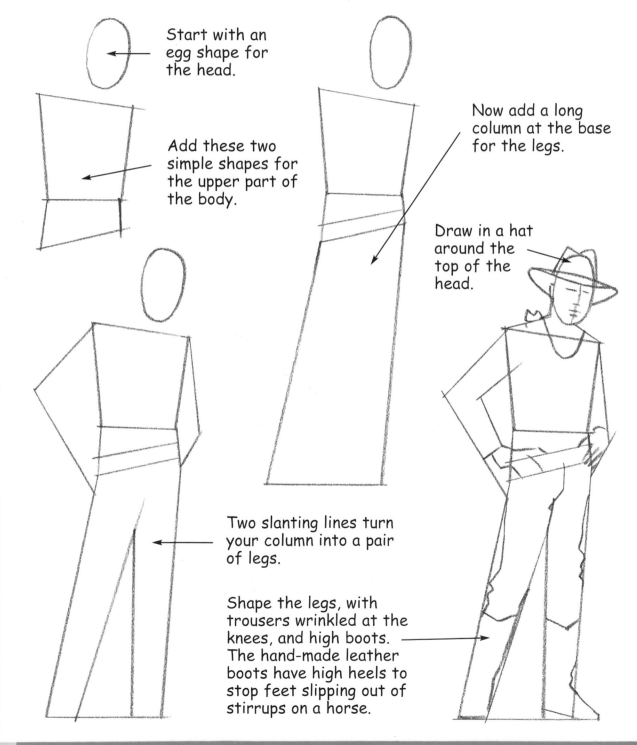

Start with an egg shape for the head.

Add these two simple shapes for the upper part of the body.

Now add a long column at the base for the legs.

Draw in a hat around the top of the head.

Two slanting lines turn your column into a pair of legs.

Shape the legs, with trousers wrinkled at the knees, and high boots. The hand-made leather boots have high heels to stop feet slipping out of stirrups on a horse.

A line sketched down the centre of the face will help you position eyes, nose and mouth.

Now draw in his clothes – jeans, shirt and a short waistcoat, or 'vest'.

A gun was protection from thieves and rustlers (cattle thieves). But long months on the trail made for short tempers, and gunfights were common.

The gunbelt is worn low on the hips, at a slant. The six-shooter gun is carried in a leather holster.

A bandanna (cotton neckcloth) protects his neck from the Sun. On cattle drives, it serves as a mask against the choking dust kicked up by the animals' feet.

The holster is tied to the thigh with a cord to stop it moving about.

The high, broad-rimmed hat keeps the head cool and shades the eyes from the Sun.

There are still cowboys today – but they tend their cattle from pick-up trucks and helicopters as well as from horses as in days gone by.

Astronaut

Out in space, an astronaut depends on his spacesuit for his life. It keeps his body at normal pressure and provides air for him to breathe.

The head and body are two rounded shapes.

This slanting four-sided shape will help you to position the arms.

Add a wide 'skirt' shape for the legs, which are spread apart.

Start shaping the arms with short straight lines.

Draw a large oval within the round helmet for the visor.

This leg is almost straight. A short line gives the other leg a bent knee.

The suit is heavily padded for protection, so the arms, legs and body look bulky.

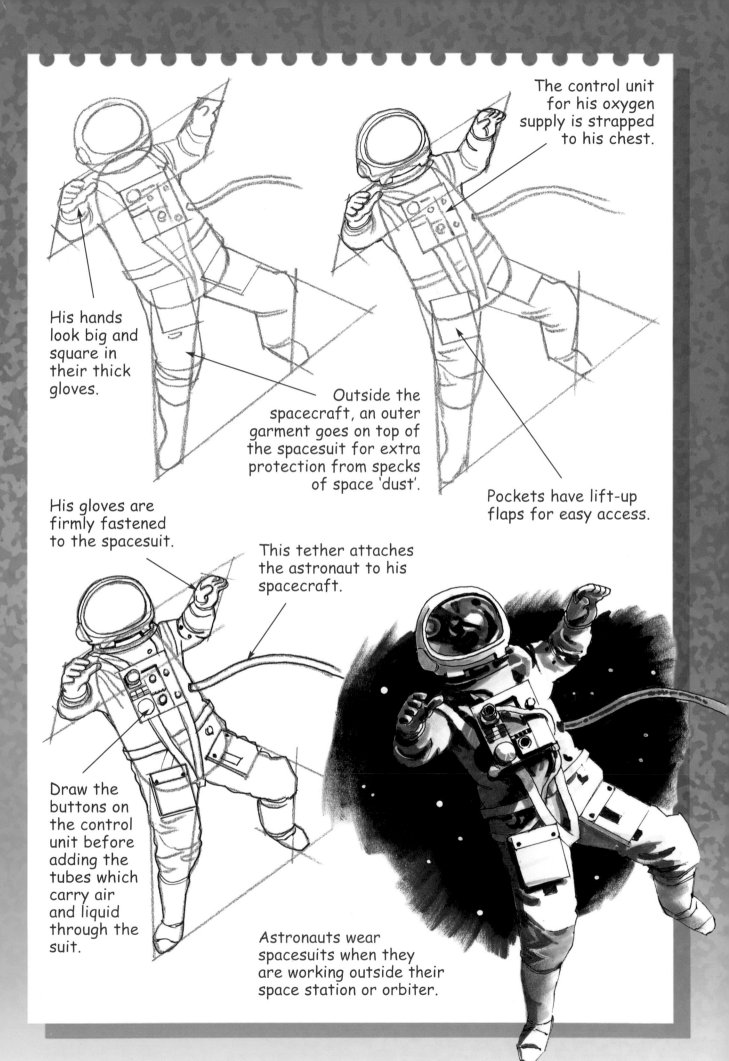

The control unit for his oxygen supply is strapped to his chest.

His hands look big and square in their thick gloves.

Outside the spacecraft, an outer garment goes on top of the spacesuit for extra protection from specks of space 'dust'.

Pockets have lift-up flaps for easy access.

His gloves are firmly fastened to the spacesuit.

This tether attaches the astronaut to his spacecraft.

Draw the buttons on the control unit before adding the tubes which carry air and liquid through the suit.

Astronauts wear spacesuits when they are working outside their space station or orbiter.

Japanese Girl

This Japanese girl is wearing her traditional costume, a loose, long-sleeved gown called a kimono. This graceful garment is worn both by men and women. The wide sash at the waist, called an obi, is also traditional.

Start with an egg shape for the head, on a thick, slanting stem – not a lopsided neck, but part of the shoulder!

Add a long column, wider at the bottom, for the floor-length kimono.

These two blocks form one of the wide sleeves.

Draw a large oval behind her head, reaching down to her waist, for her parasol, or sunshade.

Draw a 'halo' around her head. This forms the outline of her hair.

This chunky shape behind her arm is part of the sash, tied in a bulky bow behind her back.

At the end of the sleeve, draw this small shape for her hand.

Change the straight line at the bottom of the robe into a wavy edge. This helps to suggest the way the material hangs in folds.

Draw in the slender ribs of her delicate paper parasol.

A folded fan is held in her right hand, ready for graceful use.

Her kimono hangs in soft folds, shown by pencil lines. Be sure to match these up with the curves of the hem.

Ink in the parasol struts lightly. When you colour in your drawing, you may want to add painted leaves or flowers on the open sunshade.

The obi (sash) is often beautifully embroidered.

Nowadays, more and more Japanese wear Western-style clothing rather than beautiful kimonos like this.

She wears a simple sandal, and a divided sock which separates the big toe from the other toes.

Firefighter

The first organized team of firefighters was formed by the Ancient Romans. Regular fire brigades were not formed until the 18th century. Today they use modern equipment, but theirs is still a very dangerous job.

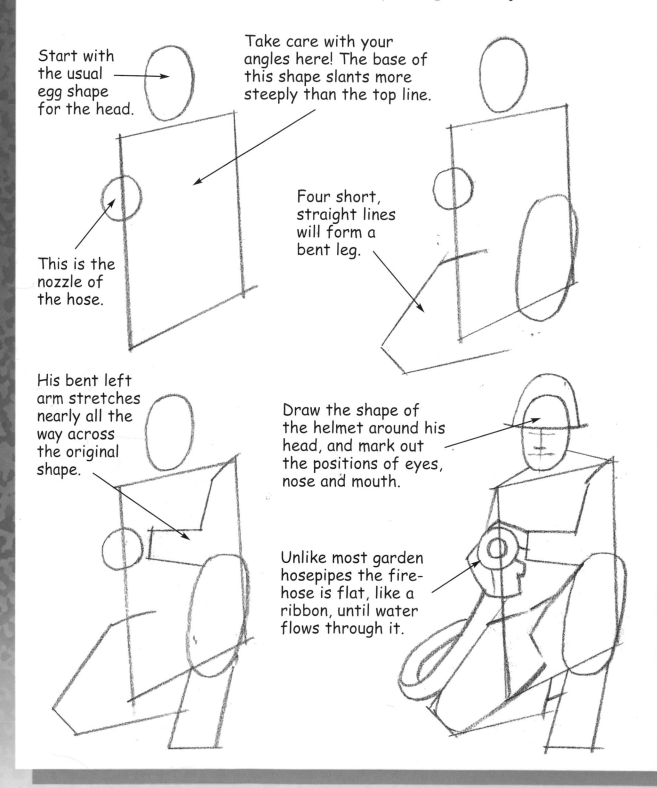

Start with the usual egg shape for the head.

Take care with your angles here! The base of this shape slants more steeply than the top line.

This is the nozzle of the hose.

Four short, straight lines will form a bent leg.

His bent left arm stretches nearly all the way across the original shape.

Draw the shape of the helmet around his head, and mark out the positions of eyes, nose and mouth.

Unlike most garden hosepipes the fire-hose is flat, like a ribbon, until water flows through it.

Draw in his protective jacket, with its turned-up collar.

This 'splash suit' is the outfit worn for most fires. It is made of heat-resistant materials developed for spaceflight.

The hard helmet protects the firefighter's head from falling debris.

The long jacket and high-waisted trousers keep him dry as well as protecting him from searing heat.

Heavy boots are essential.

Water is pumped down the hose with such force that it may take several firefighters to control the nozzle.

For dangerous situations like aircraft fuel fires, a fire-resistant suit is worn over the splash suit. Firefighters also have chemical protection suits for fires involving poisonous chemicals.

Tennis Player

The game of tennis was developed in 15th century France when it was played indoors. The outdoors version, lawn tennis, became popular in the 19th century, when the modern rules were drawn up.

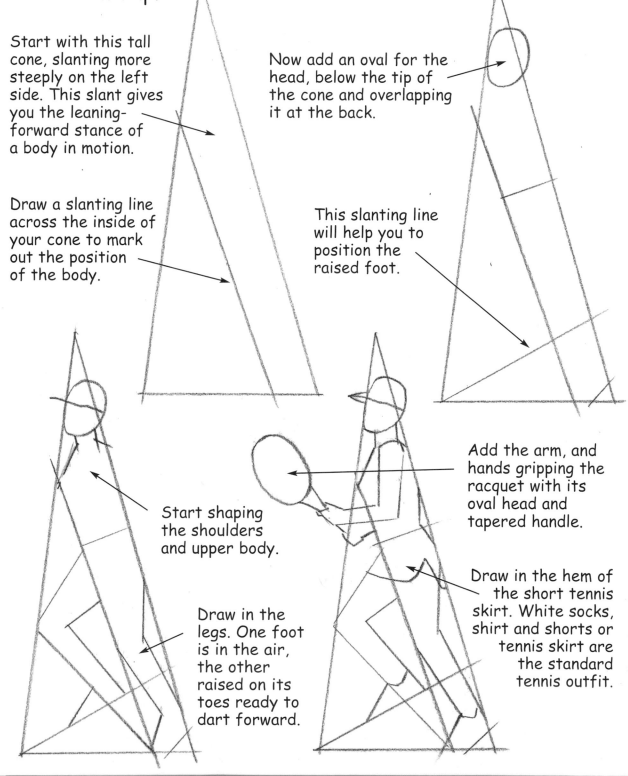

Start with this tall cone, slanting more steeply on the left side. This slant gives you the leaning-forward stance of a body in motion.

Draw a slanting line across the inside of your cone to mark out the position of the body.

Now add an oval for the head, below the tip of the cone and overlapping it at the back.

This slanting line will help you to position the raised foot.

Start shaping the shoulders and upper body.

Draw in the legs. One foot is in the air, the other raised on its toes ready to dart forward.

Add the arm, and hands gripping the racquet with its oval head and tapered handle.

Draw in the hem of the short tennis skirt. White socks, shirt and shorts or tennis skirt are the standard tennis outfit.

Draw in the face and hair.

A baseball cap shades the player's eyes from the Sun.

Start to ink in your outlines carefully.

Early racquet frames were made of wood, often ash. Nowadays modern materials like fibreglass or carbon graphite are used.

Draw the racquet strings with fine, criss-crossed lines.

Tennis shoes support the ankles and cushion the soles of the feet.

The most famous tennis championships in the world are the All-England Championships held at Wimbledon. They were first played there in 1877.

Inline Skater

Ice skates were known in ancient times. Roller skates arrived in the 18th century, fitted with wheels to glide over the ground instead of blades for skating on ice. They soon became popular worldwide. Inline skates were a 1980s development, faster and easier to turn.

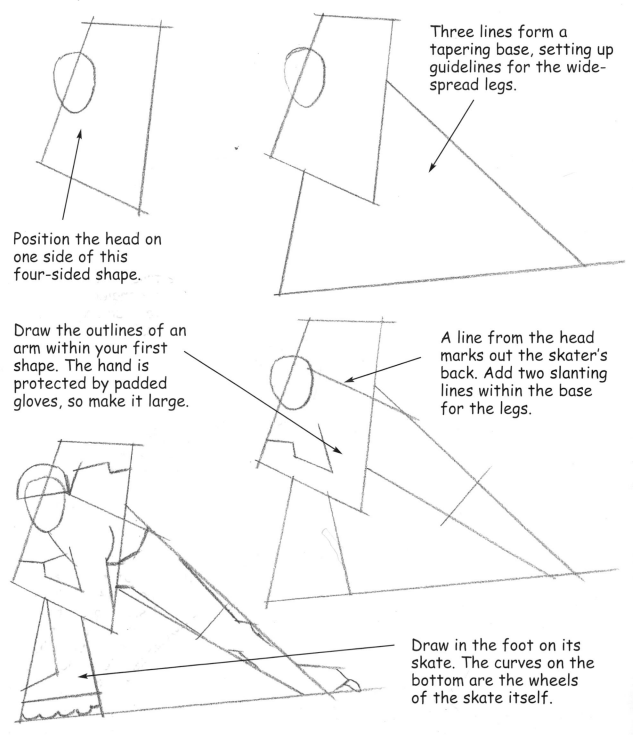

Three lines form a tapering base, setting up guidelines for the wide-spread legs.

Position the head on one side of this four-sided shape.

Draw the outlines of an arm within your first shape. The hand is protected by padded gloves, so make it large.

A line from the head marks out the skater's back. Add two slanting lines within the base for the legs.

Draw in the foot on its skate. The curves on the bottom are the wheels of the skate itself.

Use the top of your first shape as guidelines for the second arm, which is stretched up and back for balance.

Shape this outstretched leg, drawing in protective knee-pads and the lines of the skates.

The high speed of inline skates mean that falls can be nasty. So the skater's hands and elbows, as well as his knees, are protected by pads, and he wears a helmet.

The four wheels of the skate are set in a straight line rather like the blade of an ice skate.

The twisted body and sharply angled legs help to give your drawing an impression of speed.

Inline skaters have their own sports. As well as speed-skating contests, they may play roller hockey, or compete in roller derbies held on a banked track.

Ballet Dancer

Ballet dancing may express a mood, or it may tell a story, like a play using dance instead of words. It is hard work: ballet dancers practise every day to make their bodies strong and supple.

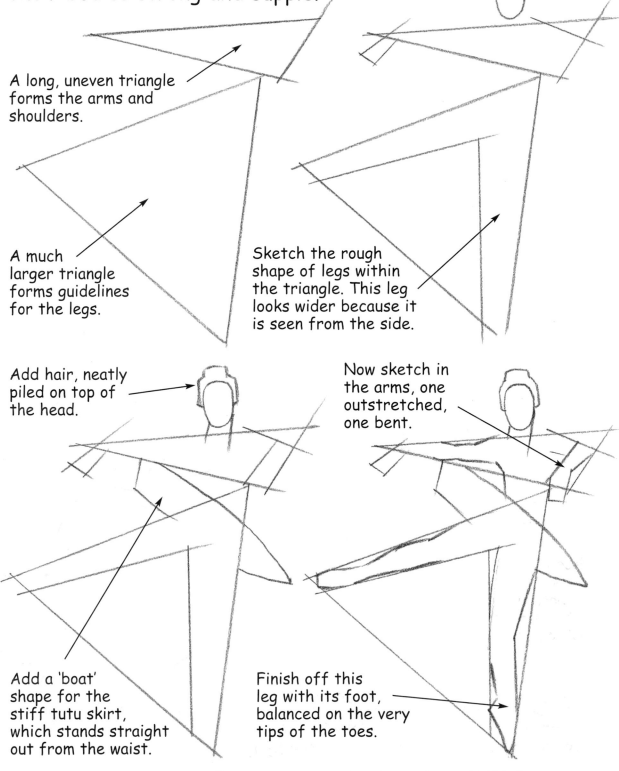

A long, uneven triangle forms the arms and shoulders.

A much larger triangle forms guidelines for the legs.

Sketch the rough shape of legs within the triangle. This leg looks wider because it is seen from the side.

Add hair, neatly piled on top of the head.

Now sketch in the arms, one outstretched, one bent.

Add a 'boat' shape for the stiff tutu skirt, which stands straight out from the waist.

Finish off this leg with its foot, balanced on the very tips of the toes.

Use a wiggly line to draw the frilled edges of the short stiff skirt.

The flowing line of the arm ends in a relaxed, gently drooping hand.

This leg turns outwards at the hip joint. The foot follows the line of the leg, with the toes pointed.

This leg is straight and fully extended, with the body fully raised on the toes of this foot.

Nearly all ballet steps are based on just five foot positions.

Dancing on the ends of the toes ('point work' or 'toe dancing') is a special technique. Special blocked shoes, strengthened at the tips, make it possible, but it is still very hard on the feet.

Native American

Western films and novels have made the 'Red Indian' brave in his feathered war headdress or 'bonnet' the best-known image of Native Americans. But these people were hunters and farmers as well as brave warriors.

Start with this tall column, divided almost down the centre.

Split the left side into three unequal sections, for head, body and legs. Draw in shapes for the arm and legs and add a circle for the war bonnet decoration.

The right side is taken up by the magnificent war bonnet, made from eagles' tail feathers. Such bonnets had to be earned by courage: each feather stood for one brave deed.

His clothes are made of the skins of buffalo, moose or elk, worked by his wives until the leather is soft. Buckskin shirts are as soft and white as silk.

He holds a war club, made of wood and stone bound with leather. This is a weapon for close combat. He might also have chosen a tomahawk. For a longer range, bow and arrows would be used.

Both men and women wore clothes decorated with patterns of stitched or woven beads. These might be made from porcupine quills, coloured with plant dyes, or glass beads imported from Europe.

Leather fringes on sleeves and hems are not just decorative, but protect the edges of clothes.

Today, most Native Americans wear Western-style clothes. You would normally only see this sort of outfit at tourist events.

His moccasins (soft leather shoes) are comfortable but not hard-wearing.

Martial Arts Expert

Martial arts are Eastern fighting skills, such as judo, karate and tae kwon do. They are intended for self-defence, not attack, and are often linked with religion. They are now also popular in the West, chiefly as sports.

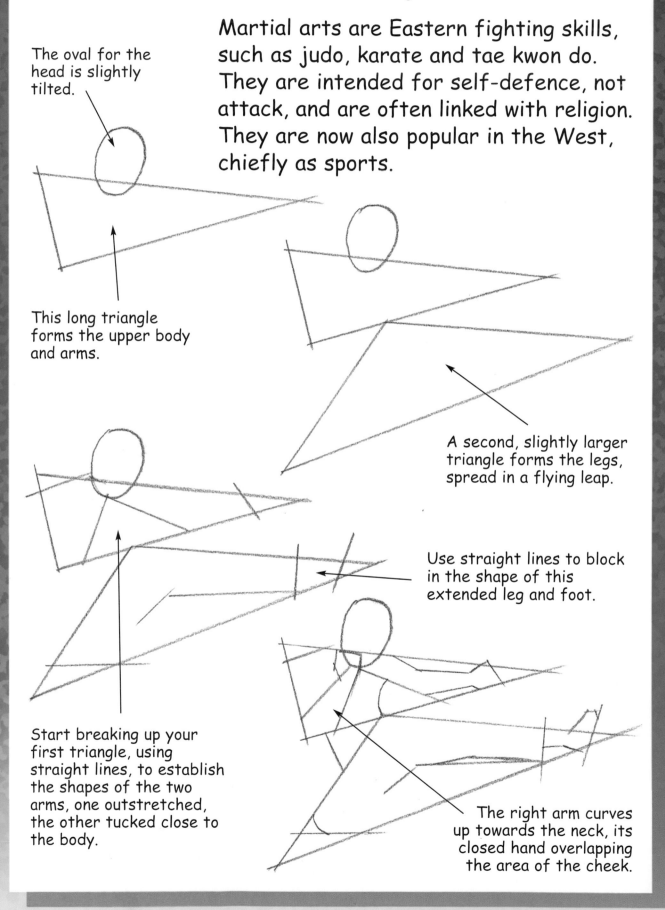

The oval for the head is slightly tilted.

This long triangle forms the upper body and arms.

A second, slightly larger triangle forms the legs, spread in a flying leap.

Use straight lines to block in the shape of this extended leg and foot.

Start breaking up your first triangle, using straight lines, to establish the shapes of the two arms, one outstretched, the other tucked close to the body.

The right arm curves up towards the neck, its closed hand overlapping the area of the cheek.

Blows with the hand are delivered with the fist, knuckles, fingertips or even palm – unlike boxing, where only the fist is used.

The arm (wrist, forearm and elbow) is used both to deliver blows and to block blows from an opponent.

The coloured belt shows the degree of skill achieved. A white belt usually means a learner, a black belt an expert. Different colours may be used to signify the levels between these.

Feet are used as well as hands to deliver blows and block an attack. The whole body follows behind a flying kick like this.

Many people enjoy practising martial arts as competitive sports. Others develop their skills to increase self-confidence and physical fitness, or as a form of self-expression, much like dancing.

Guardsman

Guards troops started out as the personal bodyguards of royalty. Today, the Guards are the 'crack' regiments of the British Army. This soldier is a member of the Household Cavalry and would be mounted on horseback for ceremonial occasions.

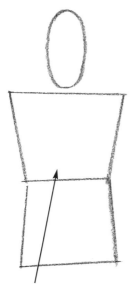

Draw the body in two sections, divided at the waist.

All Guardsmen have to be tall, and the helmet with its crest and horsehair plume adds to their height.

Draw in the arms. The hands are clasped together at waist level where they rest on the Guardsman's sword.

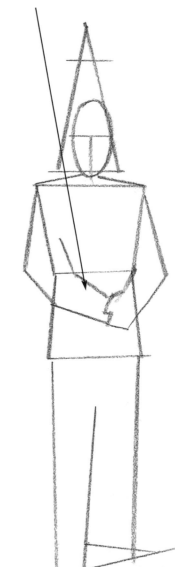

This column for the legs is longer than the body.

Start drawing in the sash, epaulettes (shoulder decorations) and other details of the uniform.

A moustache, though not essential, is part of military tradition. At one time, French hussars unable to grow a moustache had to paint one on with boot polish!

The hands, in long gloves called gauntlets, rest on the hilt of the sword.

Add some wavy edges to make the sleeves and trouser legs look more realistic.

Uniform decorations are often reminders of old customs. For example, the cord down the centre of the shoulder belt, now only decorative, used to carry a powder flask for priming guns.

A magnificent formal uniform like this is only worn on special occasions, like the Trooping The Colour celebrations on the Queen's birthday.

The long boots reach the thighs. They are called Wellingtons after the Duke of Wellington, who introduced them.

Scuba Diver

Scuba divers can swim underwater as freely as fish. They don't have to keep returning to the surface to breathe, nor are they linked to their boats by air hoses or lines. They carry their air under the water with them, in tanks strapped to their backs, and breathe it in through a mouthpiece.

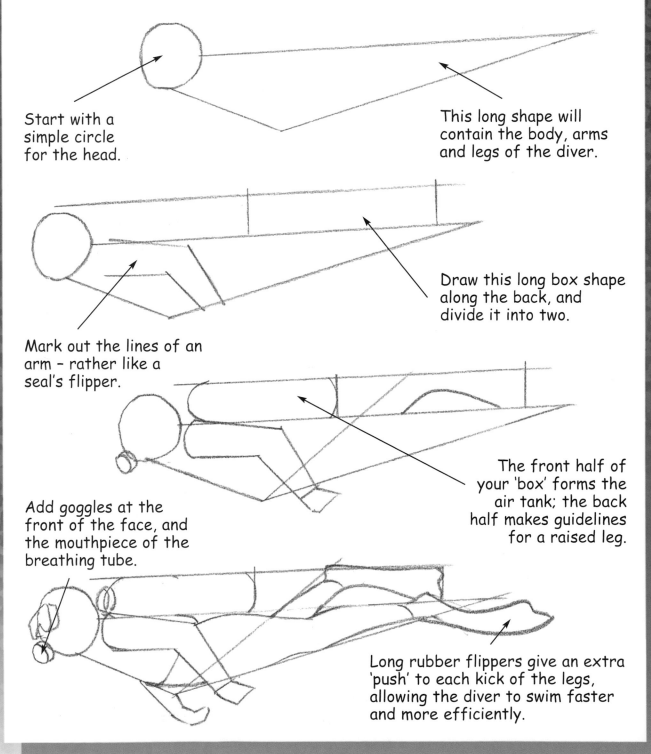

Start with a simple circle for the head.

This long shape will contain the body, arms and legs of the diver.

Draw this long box shape along the back, and divide it into two.

Mark out the lines of an arm – rather like a seal's flipper.

The front half of your 'box' forms the air tank; the back half makes guidelines for a raised leg.

Add goggles at the front of the face, and the mouthpiece of the breathing tube.

Long rubber flippers give an extra 'push' to each kick of the legs, allowing the diver to swim faster and more efficiently.

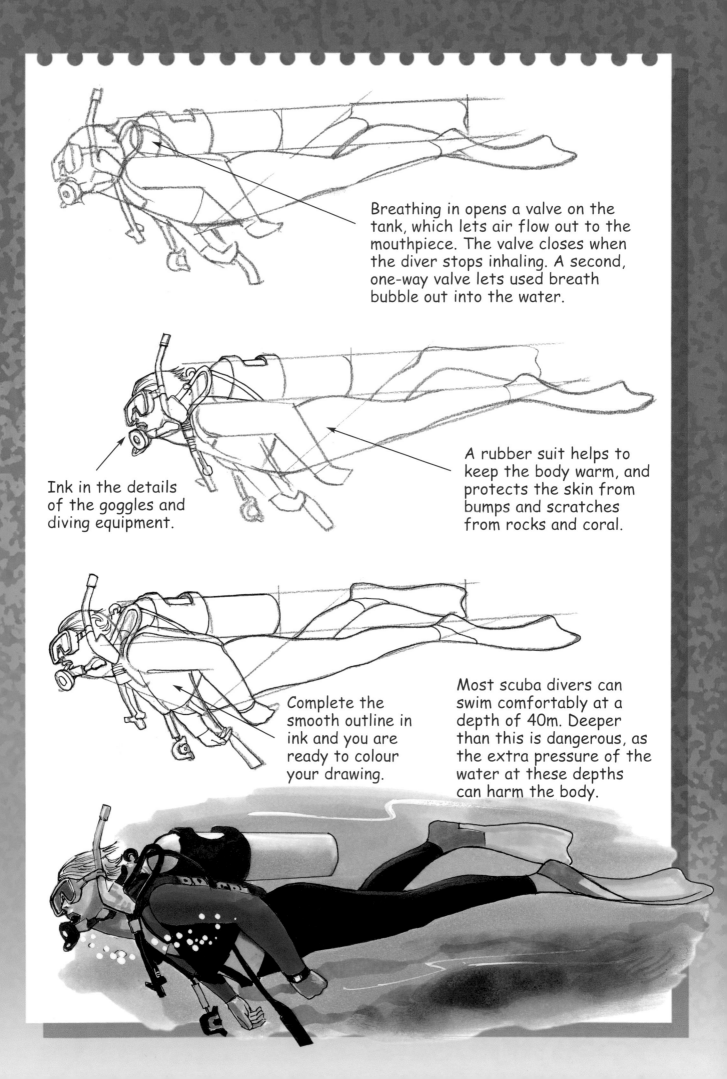

Breathing in opens a valve on the tank, which lets air flow out to the mouthpiece. The valve closes when the diver stops inhaling. A second, one-way valve lets used breath bubble out into the water.

Ink in the details of the goggles and diving equipment.

A rubber suit helps to keep the body warm, and protects the skin from bumps and scratches from rocks and coral.

Complete the smooth outline in ink and you are ready to colour your drawing.

Most scuba divers can swim comfortably at a depth of 40m. Deeper than this is dangerous, as the extra pressure of the water at these depths can harm the body.

Inuit Hunter

The Inuit are people of the Arctic – the icy land around the North Pole that is one of the harshest regions of the world. For thousands of years they have lived by hunting and fishing. They made skin tents for summer use, and houses of stone or even snow blocks (igloos) for winter.

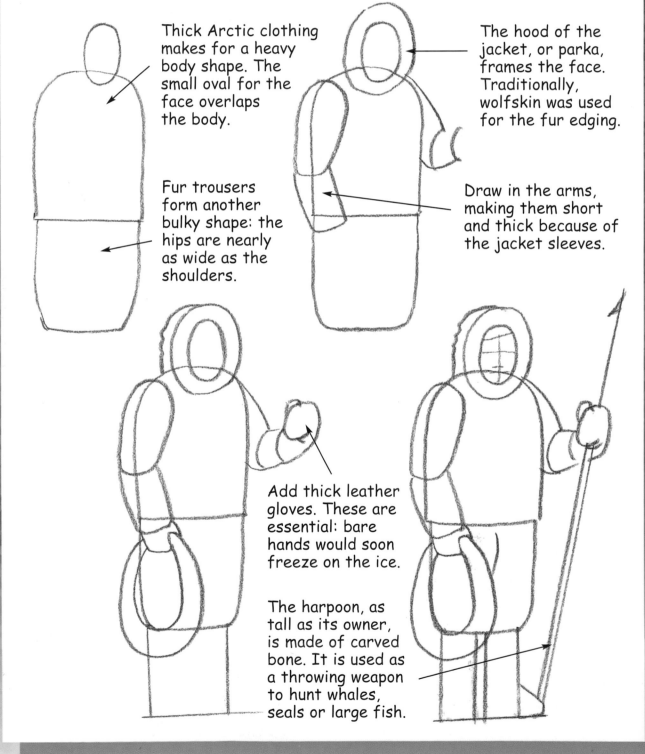

Thick Arctic clothing makes for a heavy body shape. The small oval for the face overlaps the body.

The hood of the jacket, or parka, frames the face. Traditionally, wolfskin was used for the fur edging.

Fur trousers form another bulky shape: the hips are nearly as wide as the shoulders.

Draw in the arms, making them short and thick because of the jacket sleeves.

Add thick leather gloves. These are essential: bare hands would soon freeze on the ice.

The harpoon, as tall as its owner, is made of carved bone. It is used as a throwing weapon to hunt whales, seals or large fish.

The parka has an outer layer of skins, fur side out to protect against the weather, and a lining with the fur facing inside for warmth.

The strong deerskin boots are called mukluks. Like all his clothes, they are sewn with animal sinews.

The harpoon is attached to a line, so that the catch is not lost in the water. This line is made of braided strips of sealskin.

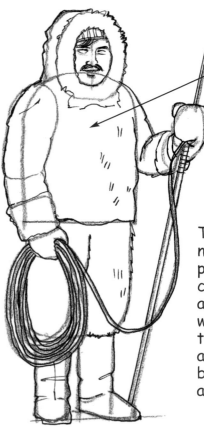

When inking in the outline of the clothes, use short jagged lines to suggest the rough texture of fur.

The Inuit wasted nothing. A seal's skin provided material for clothes, tents, boats and ropes, its bones were carved into tools and weapons, and its fat was burned for light and heat.

Scottish Piper

Everyone recognizes the kilt and tartan of Scottish national dress. Each Scottish clan (family) has its own design and colours of tartan, always forming a criss-cross pattern.

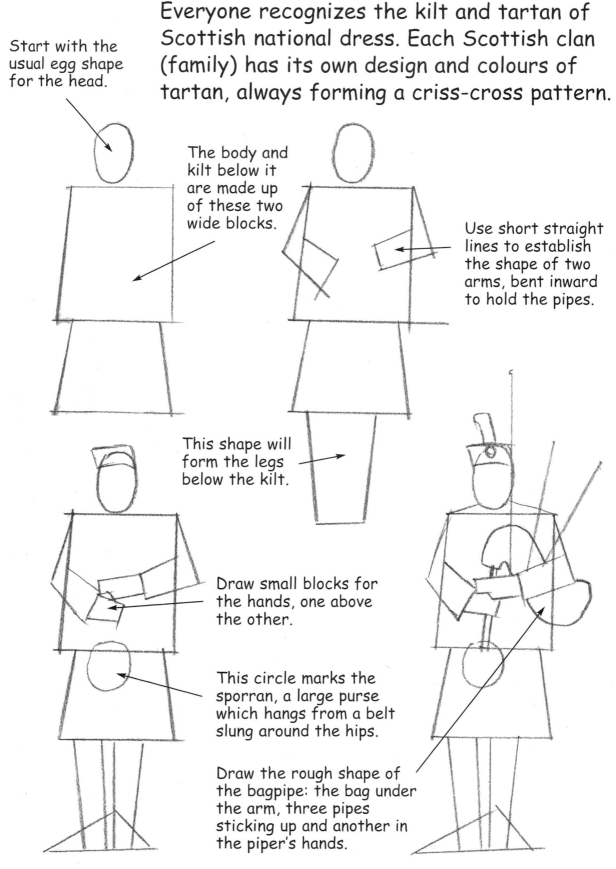

Start with the usual egg shape for the head.

The body and kilt below it are made up of these two wide blocks.

Use short straight lines to establish the shape of two arms, bent inward to hold the pipes.

This shape will form the legs below the kilt.

Draw small blocks for the hands, one above the other.

This circle marks the sporran, a large purse which hangs from a belt slung around the hips.

Draw the rough shape of the bagpipe: the bag under the arm, three pipes sticking up and another in the piper's hands.

The blow-pipe in the piper's mouth is used to fill the bag with air.

Squeezing the bag pushes air through these pipes, making a droning sound – so they are called drones.

His hands hold the melody pipe, or chanter. It has a reed and finger-holes on which the piper plays his tune.

The kilt is worn with calf-length woollen socks. A small dagger, called a dirk, may be tucked inside.

The jacket is made of tweed, a flecked woollen material. For formal occasions a black jacket is worn.

The sporran may be of plain leather with leather tassels. But more often it is decorative, trimmed with fur and silver.

Scotland's bagpipes are famous, but other countries have their own pipes too. Irish, Breton and Northumberland pipes are among the best known.